October
Patterns & Projects

Newbridge Educational Publishing, LLC
New York

© 1999 Newbridge Educational Publishing, LLC,
333 East 38th Street, New York, NY 10016. All rights reserved.

ISBN: 1-58273-126-8

10 9 8 7 6 5 4 3

Table of Contents

Table of Contents (Continued)

FIRE SAFETY BOOK

You need:
• crayons or markers
• scissors
• construction paper
• glue
• stapler

1. Reproduce the two patterns on pages 6 and 7 for each child. Have children color and cut out.
2. Distribute six sheets of construction paper to each child. Have children glue each of their patterns on separate sheets of paper.
3. On one of the remaining sheets of construction paper, have children design a cover for their Fire Safety Book. Write the title "My Fire Safety Book" on the board. Have children copy the title on the cover. They can add their own illustration under the title.
4. Staple the six pages of each child's book together.
5. Encourage children to add illustrations or important safety rules they have learned to the blank pages in their books.

Telephone Pattern

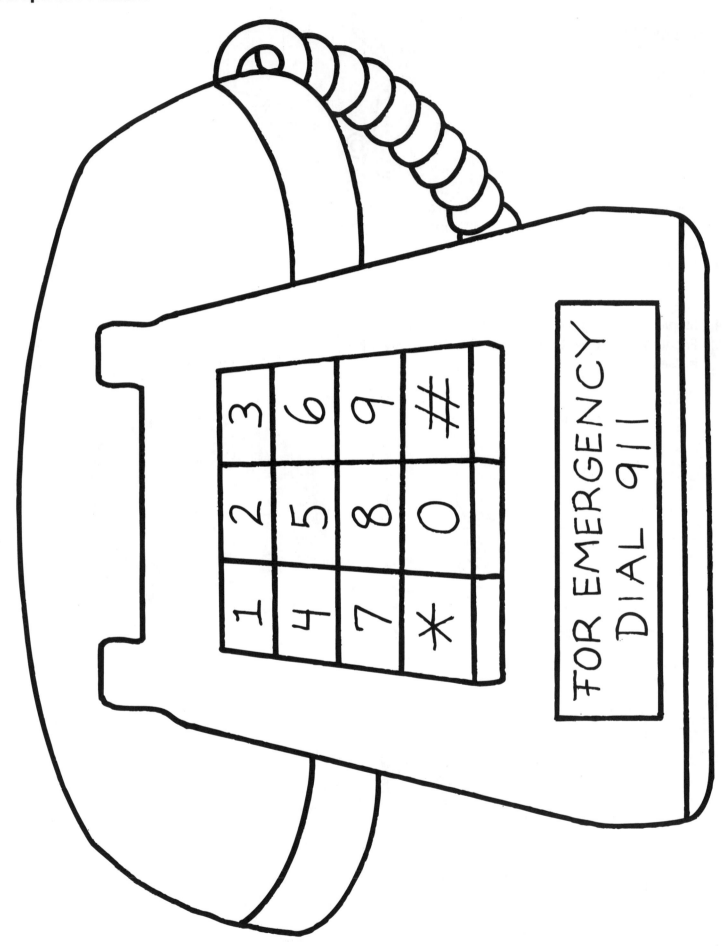

Fire Hat Pattern

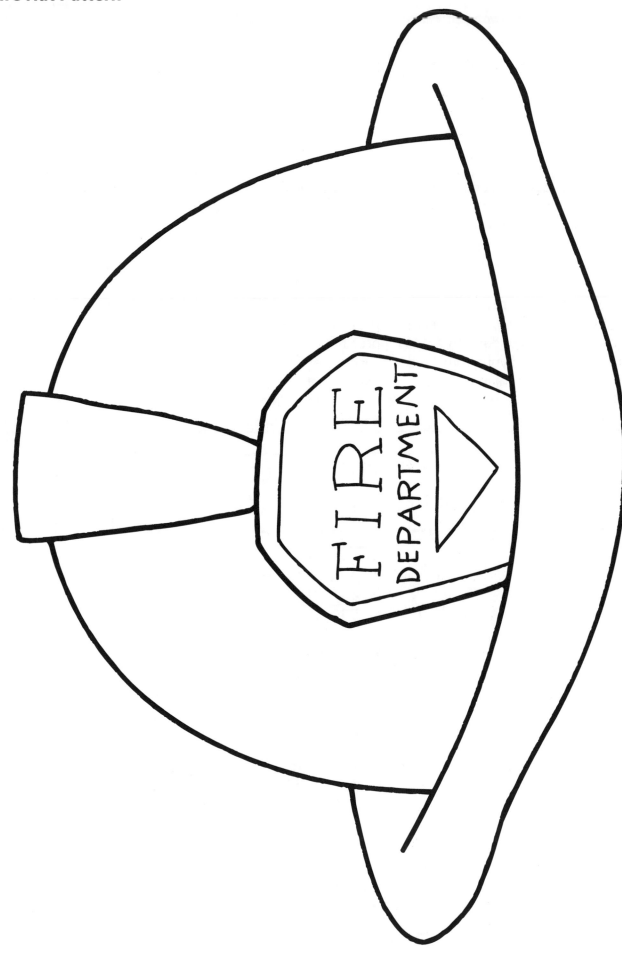

TALKING ABOUT SAFETY

You need:
• crayons or markers
• oaktag
• scissors
• glue

1. Reproduce the fire hat pattern on page 7 for each child. Have children mount on oaktag and cut out.
2. Discuss fire safety rules with the class. Encourage children to suggest dos and don'ts for fire safety. Cover points such as the following:
   • Don't ever play with matches or lighters.
   • Don't go near a stove, especially when the flame is on.
   • Don't play with electrical cords or stick anything in electrical outlets.
   • Don't leave oily rags or old papers lying around.
   • Do learn to stop, drop, and roll if your clothing ever catches fire.
   • Do learn how to call the fire department to report a fire.
   • Do learn how to get out of your home and school in case of fire.
3. Have children each write or dictate a fire safety rule on their fire hat pattern.
4. Display all fire hats on the classroom wall under the heading "Hats Off to Fire Safety!"
5. Encourage children to add their safety rules to their fire safety books.

FIRE SAFETY

Name _____

Draw an arrow pointing to the fire danger in each picture.

FIREFIGHTER GROCERY-BAG COSTUME

You need:
- crayons or markers
- scissors
- large brown grocery bags
- yellow and black paint
- paintbrushes
- tape
- 1" x 10" strips of blue tissue paper
- 1" x 12" strips of construction paper
- cardboard paper-towel roll
- stapler

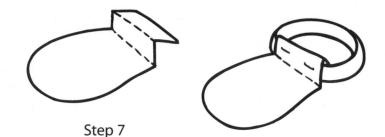

Step 7

1. Reproduce the hat pattern on pages 12 and 13 once for each child. Reproduce the boot pattern on page 14 twice for each child. Have children color and cut out.
2. Give each child one large brown grocery bag and have him or her paint it yellow. When each bag is dry, paint a black stripe around the width of the bag, as shown.
3. Help each child cut slits up the sides of the bag, as shown, to allow room for arms. Then cut a large circle from the bottom of the bag for the child's head to fit through.
4. To make the hat, have each child cut along the dotted lines and tape the two sides of the hat together. Then fold the front of each hat up, as shown.
5. To make a hose, ask each child to tape 1" x 10" strips of blue tissue paper to the inner edge of a cardboard paper-towel roll, as shown.
6. Give each child two 1" x 12" strips of construction paper. Staple the strips loosely around each child's ankles.
7. Have children fold the boots on the dotted lines and staple to the construction paper strips, as shown.
8. For activities, see Putting Out the Fire Action Song on page 15.

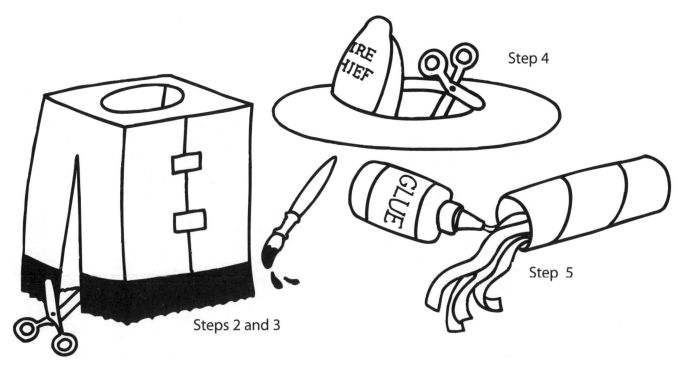

Steps 2 and 3

Step 4

Step 5

STOP, DROP, AND ROLL RELAY RACE

1. Divide children into teams of five or six. Choose one child on each team to be the leader.
2. To start the race, the leader calls out "Let's roll!" The first players on each team then run to the back of the room, stop, drop to the ground, and roll over. The players then run back to their teams and tag the next player, who repeats the action.
3. The team who completes the "stop, drop, and roll" first and sits down in place is the winner.

FIRE DRILL RELAY RACE

1. Divide the class into teams of three. Have each team choose a leader.
2. Place the three pieces of a firefighter costume at the end of the room opposite each line, one for each team.
3. To start the race, the leader calls "Fire, fire!" The first player on each team runs to the end of the room, puts on one piece of the costume, and runs back to his or her team.
4. The first player then takes off that piece of the costume and hands it to the next player. That player puts on what the first player gave him or her, runs down to the end, and puts on another piece of the costume.
5. The last player puts on both pieces given to him or her by the second player, runs to the end and puts on the last piece, and runs back to his or her team.
6. The team whose last player returns first wins.

Fire Hat Pattern

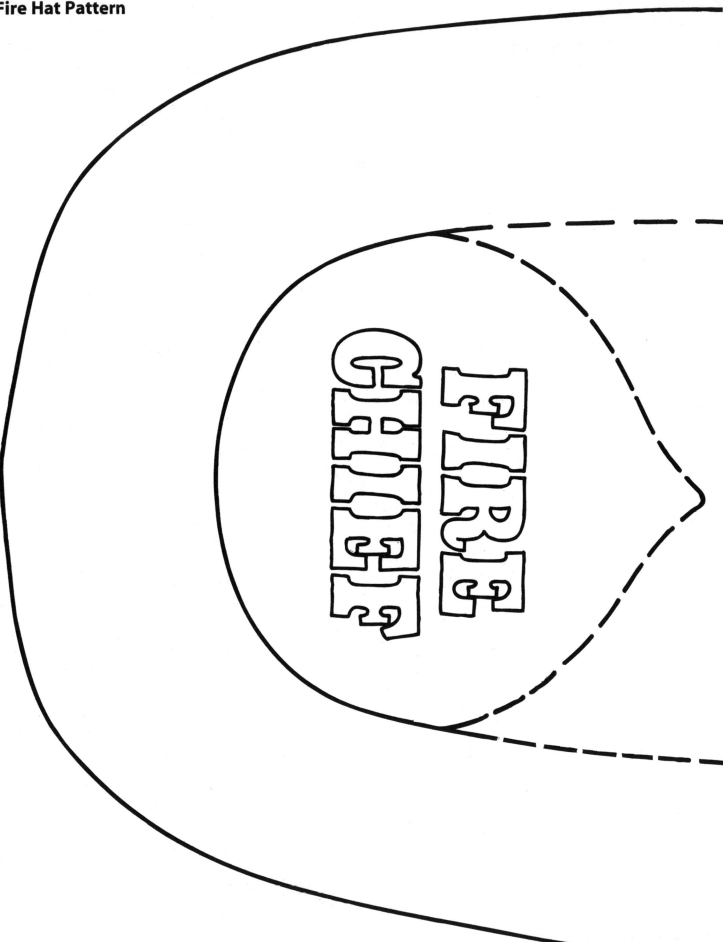

Fire Hat Pattern

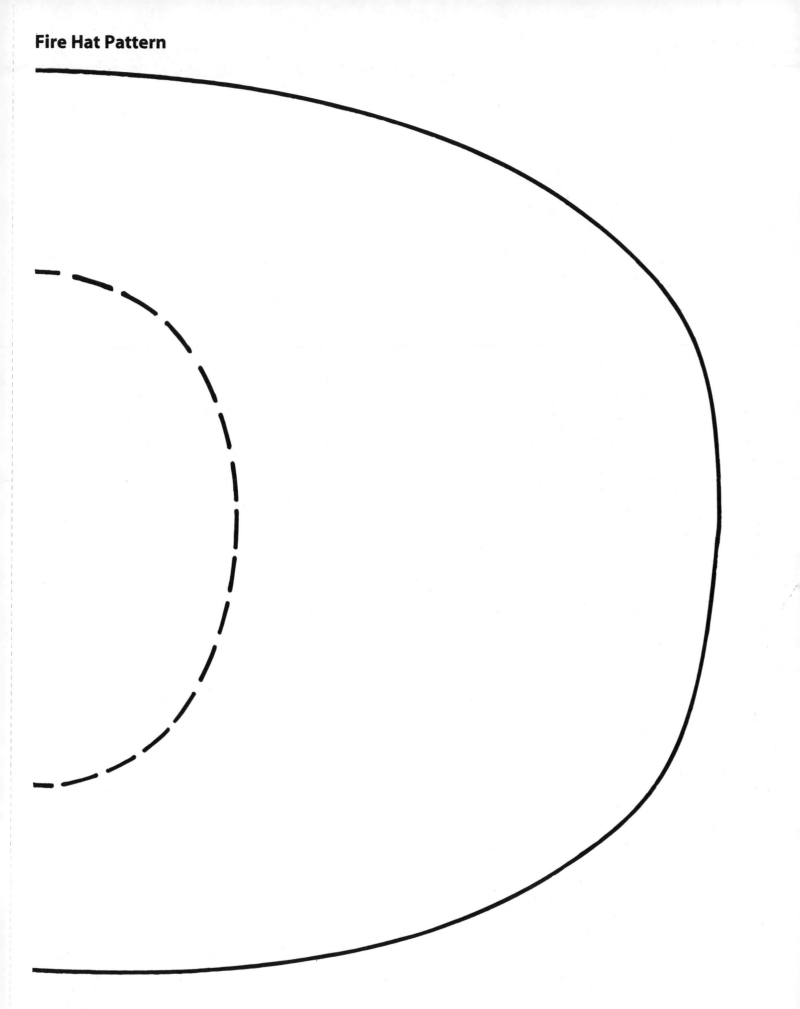

Fire Boot Pattern

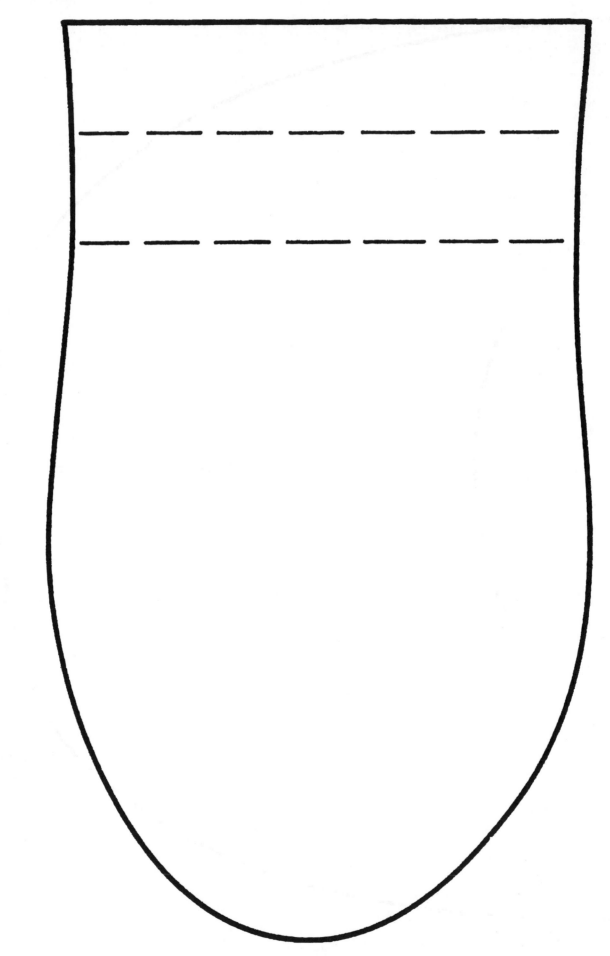

PUTTING OUT THE FIRE ACTION SONG
(sung to the tune of "Miss Lucy")

Teach children the following song about firefighters. Have children wear their firefighter costumes and act out the words as they sing.

Firefighter riding
In your truck so high.
Going to a fire,
Racing right on by.
Spray water on the fire
Until it goes away.
Firefighters keep us safe,
Every night and day.

My friend once saw a fire.
She called up 911.
They rang the little firehouse.
The truck came on the run.

"Sizzle!" went the fire.
"Oooh!" said the crowd.
"Back," said the firefighter,
Who had to speak so loud.

Out went the fire.
Home went the crowd.
Back at the firehouse
They all felt mighty proud.

FIREFIGHTER CLASS DISCUSSION

Take children on a visit to the neighborhood firehouse, or have firefighters visit the classroom. Encourage children to ask questions about the truck, the protective outfit firefighters wear, what a fire is like, how they put out fires, and what they do at the firehouse when not on a call.

When you return to the classroom, review the things children learned from the firefighters. Write down children's comments on an experience chart. Then have the class practice the "stop, drop, and roll" technique and explain to them why it is an important thing to remember.

Help children make child alert signs for their bedroom windows at home. Give each child a piece of white construction paper. Have children draw pictures showing sleeping children. Tell children to label the signs "Child Inside." Each child should ask his or her parents' permission to tape the sign to a window where it can be spotted easily by firefighters in case of fire.

RECOMMENDED READING

Read the following books about firefighters to your class. Place the books on a reading table or in a bookcase so that children may look at them during free time.

Country Fireman by Jerrold Beim, published by William Morrow.
The Fire Cat by Esther Averill, published by HarperCollins
Fire Fighting in America by Alfred Tamarin, published by Macmillan
Here Comes the Fireboat by Lillian Colonius and Glenn Schroeder, published by Elk Grove Press.
I Know a Fireman by Barbara Williams, published by Putnam.
Let's Go to a Firehouse by Naomi Buycheimer, published by Putnam.

COLUMBUS DAY FLANNEL BOARD

You need:
• crayons or markers
• glue
• scissors
• oaktag
• flannel for a flannel board
• scraps of flannel or sandpaper

1. Reproduce the Columbus, King Ferdinand, and Queen Isabella patterns on page 20 once. Reproduce the ship on page 19 three times, and the sailors and Native American patterns on page 21 several times. Have children color, mount on oaktag, and cut out.
2. Glue scraps of flannel or sandpaper to the back of each cutout.
3. Prepare a large flannel board on which to stick the patterns.
4. Have volunteers move the patterns around the board as you read the story of Columbus aloud.
5. During free time, let children play with the flannel board to create their own stories featuring characters from the story of Columbus.

COLUMBUS DAY FLANNEL BOARD STORY

Over 500 years ago, in the year 1451, Christopher Columbus was born in Genoa, Italy. Genoa is a city that lies on the sea. As a child, young Christopher often went down to the seaport and watched the sailors come and go on their boats and ships. Sometimes he was even let on board, and he learned how to handle oars and sail on water.

More than anything, Christopher Columbus dreamed of becoming a sailor himself. He got his first chance when he was about 20 years old, but the trip nearly cost him his life. During the voyage, the boat was attacked by enemy sailors. Christopher had to jump into the water to save his life. He held onto an oar as a life preserver until reaching land.

But this bad experience did not discourage Columbus from wanting to be a sailor. A few years later, Columbus moved to Spain. He became more and more interested in sailing, wondering what places he might find on his travels. At this time, other sailors were wondering the same thing. They wanted to find a shorter way to get from Spain to the Indies , which included China, Japan, and India. Ships from the Indies brought back gold, gems, and spices to Spain and other countries. But going between Spain and the Indies meant going many thousands of miles. The only route sailors knew at the time was to sail all the way around Africa. Christopher Columbus thought there must be a shorter way. In order to carry out his plan, Columbus needed money for ships and other equipment. He went to King Ferdinand and Queen Isabella of Spain. He told them about the voyage he wanted to take to find a shortcut to the Indies. At first, the King and Queen were not persuaded, but finally Columbus convinced them, and they gave him money to pay for his trip.

The year was 1492, and Columbus was ready to set sail. He had three ships, called the Niña, the Pinta, and the Santa Maria. About 90 sailors joined Columbus on the ships. On August 3, 1492, Columbus and his crew left Spain. The men had compasses, but their instruments were not very accurate. Columbus used the sun and the stars to help guide him toward the Indies. He headed straight west. The voyage across the sea was not an easy one. Although the weather was good most of the time, many crew members began to worry that the wind would blow them in the wrong direction. After sailing for three weeks without seeing land, the sailors tried to persuade Columbus to turn back and go home. But Columbus refused. Finally, on October 12, the nervous crew was relieved to spot land. The ships landed and the sailors planted flags, claiming the land for the King and Queen of Spain.

On land, Columbus met many people he had never heard of before. Columbus thought he had reached the Indies, so he called the people "Indians." What Columbus didn't realize was that he had not reached the Indies at all. Instead, he had landed in a place no one in Spain even knew existed. Today, that land is called America.

After searching for gold and gems in America, Columbus returned to Spain. Later, Columbus made three more trips to America. Although he never found a shortcut to the Indies, he did find a land that other Europeans then began to travel to and explore.

Christopher Columbus is now famous around the world, and in his honor Columbus Day is observed every year in October.

Ship Pattern

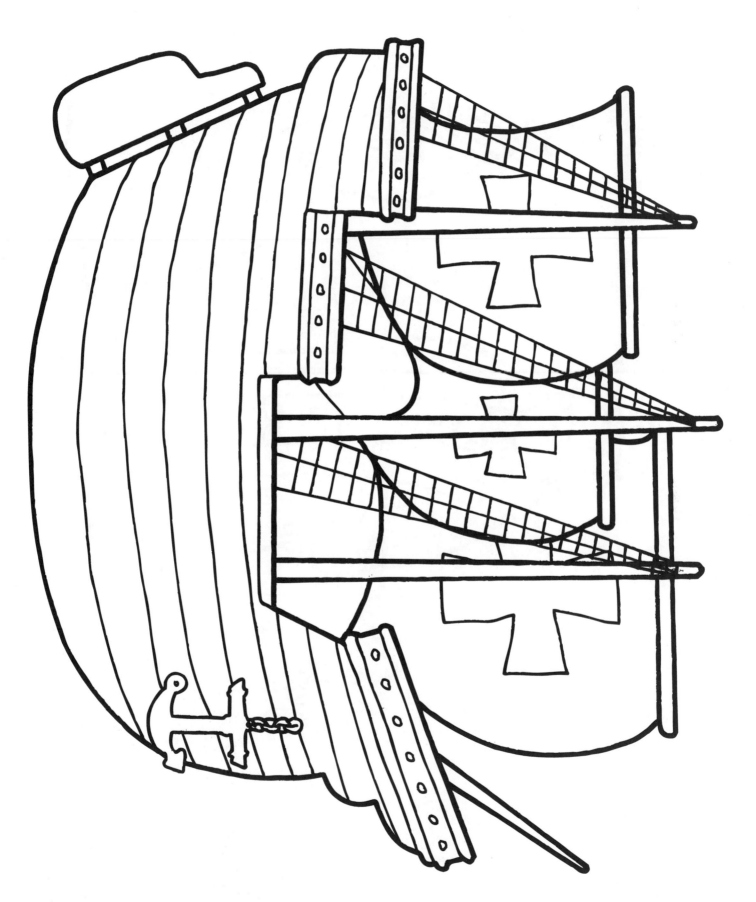

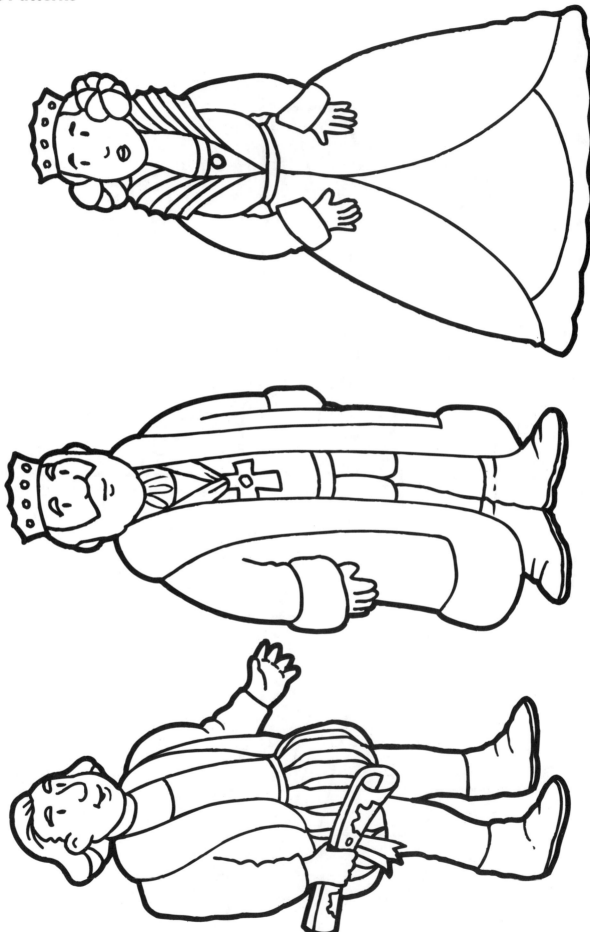

Columbus Patterns

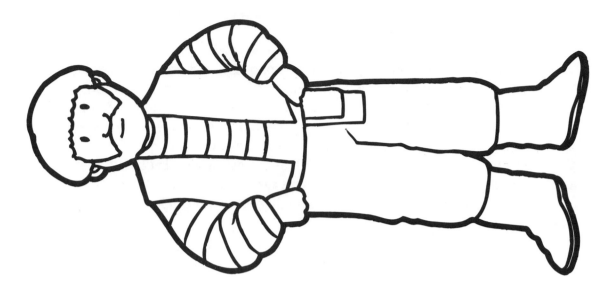

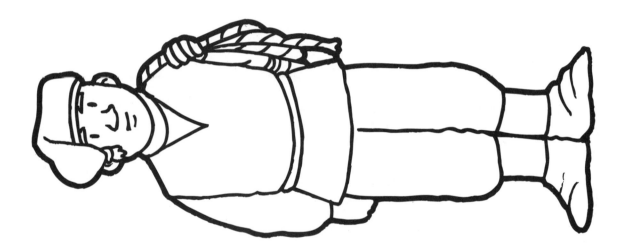

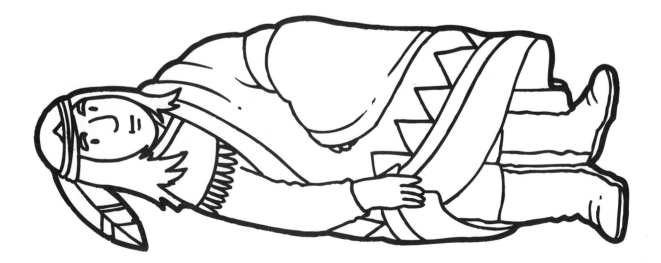

COLUMBUS DAY CLASS DISCUSSION

1. Point out each figure on the Columbus Day mobile (see page 23) and explain its significance: the ships were called the Niña, the Pinta, and the Santa Maria; the explorer was Christopher Columbus, who landed close to the North American mainland; and the sailors helped sail the ships and watch for land.
2. Ask children how they would feel if they were on a ship and didn't see any land for weeks and weeks. What would they do all day? What would they eat? Where could they go?
3. Compare Columbus with modern-day explorers, such as our astronauts. Explain that astronauts in space probably feel much the same way Columbus felt on his explorations.
4. Ask children to predict what some future explorers might find. Write children's predictions on a large piece of oaktag under the title "Adventures of the Future."

COLUMBUS DAY MOBILE

You need:
- crayons or markers
- scissors
- glue
- oaktag
- hole puncher
- yarn

1. Reproduce the Columbus pattern and the king and queen patterns on page 20 twice for each child. Also reproduce the ship pattern on page 19 six times and the sailor patterns on page 21 four times. Have children color and cut out.

2. Have children paste each pattern together, as shown, so they are two-sided. Show children how to punch holes in the tops of the patterns, as shown.

3. Help children thread lengths of yarn through the holes and tie.

4. Help each child punch eight holes along the bottom edge of a 3" x 30" strip of oaktag and three holes along the top, as shown. Then help them thread the yarn ends through the eight holes and tie. Staple the strip into a circle, as shown.

5. Show children how to thread three 12" lengths of yarn through the top three holes and tie. Help children bring all three pieces of yarn together on top and tie to complete the mobile.

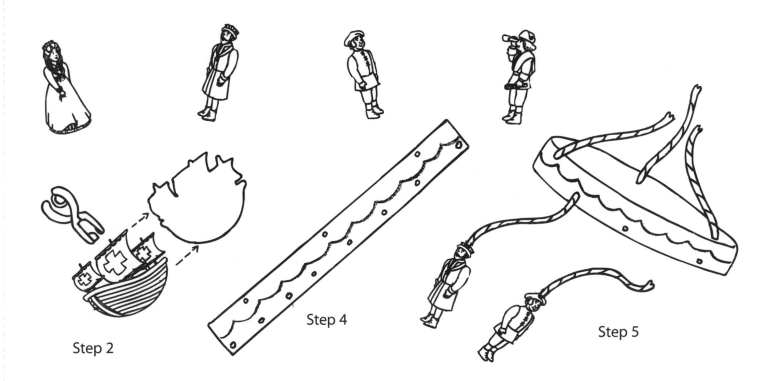

Step 2

Step 4

Step 5

23

HEADING IN THE RIGHT DIRECTION

You need:
• a world map or globe
• a compass
• large sheets of white paper
• four pieces of notebook paper
• crayons or markers
• tape

1. Use a world map or globe to show children the route that Columbus followed to get from Spain to America. Point out the directions north, south, east, and west on the map. Explain that Columbus basically sailed west to reach his destination.
2. Help children determine the directions north, south, east, and west in the classroom. If possible, bring in a compass. Let children see the four directions indicated. Have them note how the arrow points to a different direction as they turn themselves around while holding the compass.
3. Explain that directions can also be determined by noting where the sun rises and sets in the sky. The sun rises in the East and sets in the West. Let children look out the window and use the sun's position to help them determine direction.
4. Write the labels north, south, east, and west on individual pieces of notebook paper. Tape each sign on the appropriate wall in the classroom.
5. Have children work with a partner to draw their own maps of the classroom on large sheets of paper. Children should label north, south, east, and west on their maps, using the wall labels for help.
6. Use the maps to ask questions such as the following:
   "In which direction would you travel to get from the teacher's desk to the closet?"
   "If you started at the coat room and walked north, where would you end up?"

COLUMBUS DAY CARDS

You need:
• crayons or markers
• scissors
• construction paper
• glue

1. Have children each choose one pattern from pages 19 through 21 to use for the cover of their Columbus Day card. Reproduce one pattern for each child. Have children color and cut out the pattern.
2. Give each child a sheet of construction paper. Have children fold the paper to form a card, as shown. Then they glue the pattern to the front of the card.
3. Inside the card, children may add their own special message, in poetry or prose, about Columbus Day. Have children write or dictate their message.

RECOMMENDED READING

Read some of the following books about Columbus and Columbus Day to the class.
Place the books on a reading table or in a library corner so children may look at them during their free time.

All Pigs on Deck by Laura Fischetto, published by Delacorte.
Christopher Columbus by Robert Young, published by Silver Press.
Christopher Columbus: A Great Explorer by Carol Greene, published by Children's Press.
Christopher Columbus, Who Sailed On! by Dorothy Richards, published by Child's World.
The Discovery of America by Betsy Maestro, published by Lothrop, Lee & Shepard.
Follow the Dream by Peter Sis, published by Knopf.
In 1492 by Jean Marzollo, published by Scholastic.
My First Columbus Day Book by Dee Lillegard, published by Children's Press.
A Picture Book of Christopher Columbus by David Adler, published by Holiday House.
What Is Columbus Day? by Margot Parker, published by Children's Press.

COLUMBUS DAY MURAL

You need:
• crayons or markers
• scissors
• large roll of paper, such as butcher paper
• tempera or watercolor paint and brushes
• construction paper
• glue
• drinking straws (paper, if possible)

1. Reproduce one Columbus and several sailor patterns on pages 20 and 21. Have children color the figures and cut out.
2. Give a small group of children a long sheet of mural paper. Ask them to paint the paper to depict the sky and water.
3. Ask children to make ships out of construction paper by cutting half-ovals for the bottoms of the ships, and triangle sails. Have children glue the ship bottoms to the mural's ocean, attaching straws for masts, and finally gluing sails next to the straws, as shown.
4. Have children glue the sailors and Columbus figures on the ships. If desired, children can write or dictate a few sentences about Columbus's voyage.

COLUMBUS DAY ACTION STORY

Have children wear their sailor hats as they help act out this story. Suggestions for dramatizing the action are given in parentheses.

A long, long time ago a boy named Christopher Columbus wanted to be a sailor. Day and night he watched ships in the harbor. He began to sail the seas when he was a young man, and he worked very hard on the ships. When he was a little older, Columbus became the captain of a ship. He loved to study maps and think of new places he might explore.

One day Columbus went to see Queen Isabella of Spain. He asked her to give him ships and supplies so that he could sail far to the west, where no one had ever sailed before. Many people thought it was dangerous to take a ship in that direction; they were afraid of what they might find there. At first the queen did not want to grant Columbus's request. But he promised her that if he found spices, gold, and jewels, he would bring them back to her. So Queen Isabella decided to give Columbus three ships.

Columbus gathered together sailors who liked adventure as much as he did. They loaded the ships with food and fresh water for their journey. The three ships, named the Niña, the Pinta, and the Santa Maria, set sail one day in August 1492.

The three ships sailed west. There was nothing to see but ocean and sky. *(put hand to forehead and look around)* Sometimes the water sparkled and the sun shone brightly. Sometimes clouds covered the sun. And sometimes the wind blew and the rain fell. *(hug body and shiver)* But the three ships could not stop for bad weather. As the ships sailed over choppy waters, the sailors rolled back and forth on the decks. *(roll body back and forth)* To make sure that the ships stayed on their westward course, the sailors checked the stars on clear nights. *(look up at sky)* The ocean voyage lasted many, many weeks. Eventually the sailors began to complain about their life on the sea. They only had biscuits and dried beans to eat for almost all their meals. Their water, which was kept in wooden barrels, tasted bad. And they were sore from having to sleep on the hard decks. Some of the sailors wanted to turn around and go back to Spain.

Then one day the sailors shouted for joy. *(wave arms up in the air excitedly)* They pointed to the sky, and there was a bird! *(point up at the sky)* That meant the ships were near land, for birds do not fly out in the middle of the ocean. How happy the sailors were when they finally saw land. When the ships landed, the sailors jumped out and patted the ground. *(reach down and pat ground)* They looked around and noticed beautiful flowers and trees that they had never seen before. *(look all around as if in wonder)* They also noticed they were not alone. The sailors stared at the people who were watching them, and the people stared back. Columbus and the sailors called the people "Indians" because they thought they had sailed to India. They didn't see much gold, but they did find hammocks, parrots, corn, cotton, beans, and sweet potatoes. Nobody in Spain had ever seen any of those things before. And because of these discoveries and his bravery, we honor Christopher Columbus on his birthday every year.

COLUMBUS DAY ACTION STORY DISCUSSION

After you have read the action story to your class, ask children the following questions:

1. Why did Christopher Columbus become a sailor?
2. Why do you think people were afraid to sail where no one had sailed before?
3. Why did Queen Isabella let Columbus have three ships and a lot of supplies?
4. What do you think the Indians thought when they saw Columbus and his men for the first time?
5. What are some things Columbus and his men saw in the New World?
6. Would you like to be an explorer? Where would you go? (If desired, have children illustrate their ideas.)

MAKING SAILOR HATS

You need:
• crayons or markers
• scissors
• 2" x 24" strips of oaktag
• stapler

1. Reproduce the hat pattern on page 29 and the feather pattern on page 32 for each child.
2. Have children color the hats and feathers and cut out.
3. Give each child a 2" x 24" strip of oaktag to use as a headband. Staple the headband to the pleats of the hat, as shown. Then cut a slit in the headband and insert the feather, as shown.
4. Staple the headband to fit around each child's head.
5. For activities, see Columbus Day Action Story on page 27 and Navigator Game on page 30.

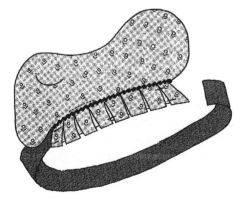

Sailor Hat Pattern

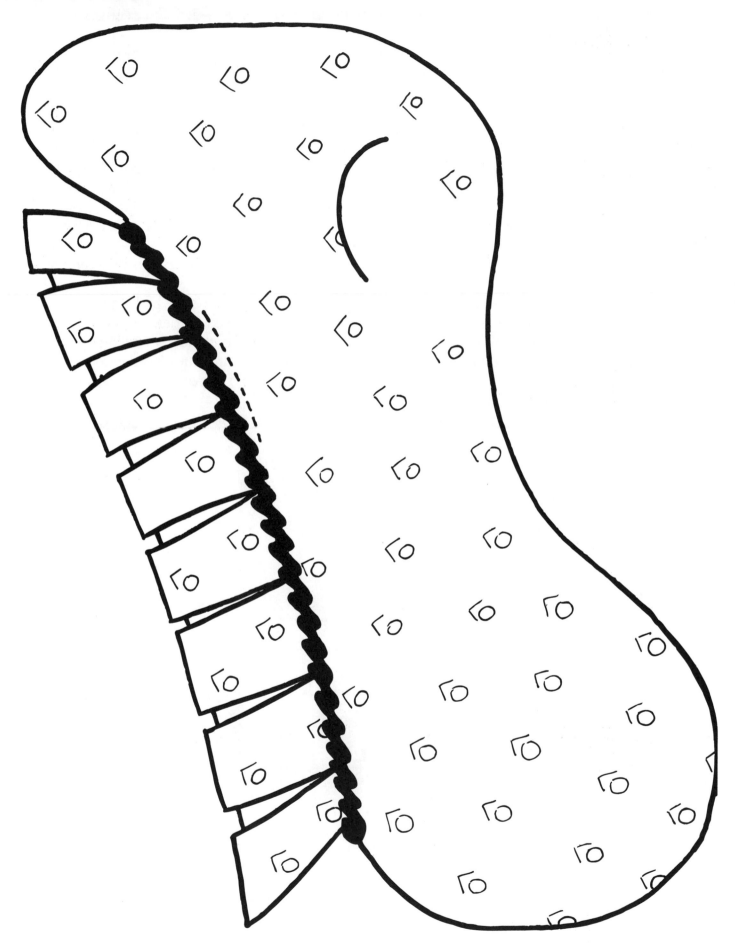

COLUMBUS DAY NAVIGATOR GAME

You need:
- 9" paper plates
- crayons or markers
- tape
- scissors
- stapler
- storybook, game, snack

1. On four paper plates, draw N (for north), S (for south), E (for east), and W (for west). Draw an arrow on each plate indicating a different direction, as shown.
2. Attach the "compasses" to the appropriate walls in the classroom. (Use a real compass to help determine the direction.)
3. Reproduce the ship patterns on pages 32 and 33 twice. Have children color the ships and cut out.
4. Put each pair of ships together and staple the pair, as shown, to make three envelopes.
5. Divide the class into three teams. Ask children to wear their sailor hats and pretend to be sailors.
6. Start the teams in the center of the room. Hand each team a ship with the first clue placed inside. (See Navigator Game Clues on page 31 for further instructions.) Help each team search for their "treasure" by reading and following the directions on their set of clues.
7. Each team should find a treasure for the whole class to enjoy, such as a storybook, a new game, or a simple snack.

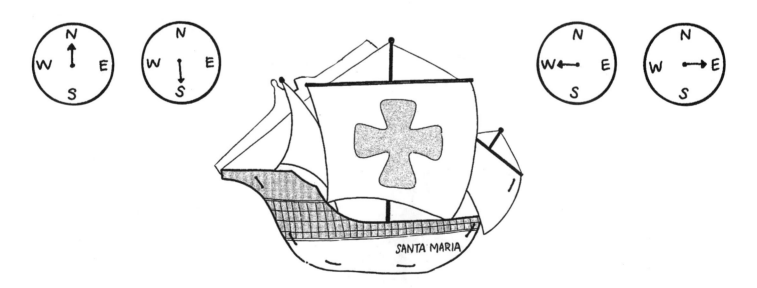

Step 4

NAVIGATOR GAME CLUES

To make the clues for the Navigator Game, write each clue on a separate index card. Write four clues for each team. Hide the treasure in the place indicated by the final clue.

1. Begin in the center of the room. Walk, using fairly small paces, to a piece of furniture. Record the number of steps needed to walk there and the direction in which the furniture lies. For example, "Walk 9 steps E." From there, walk to another piece of furniture in a different part of the room. Again, record the number of steps and the direction and write the clue. Continue doing this to create two more clues.
2. After writing the four clues for each team on index cards, place the first clue inside the team's ship and the remaining clues in their appropriate places in the room. For example:
   The Pinta team begins by looking at its first clue, which says, "Walk 9 steps E." The Pinta sailors look at the compasses, find E (for east), and proceed 9 steps in that direction. There they find a bookcase. On top of the bookcase is another clue, which says, "Walk 10 steps N." Each team continues on their search until they find their treasure.

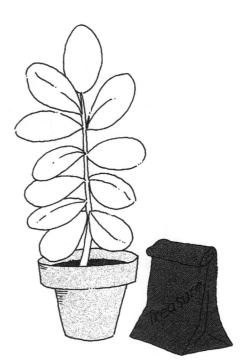

Santa Maria and Feather Patterns

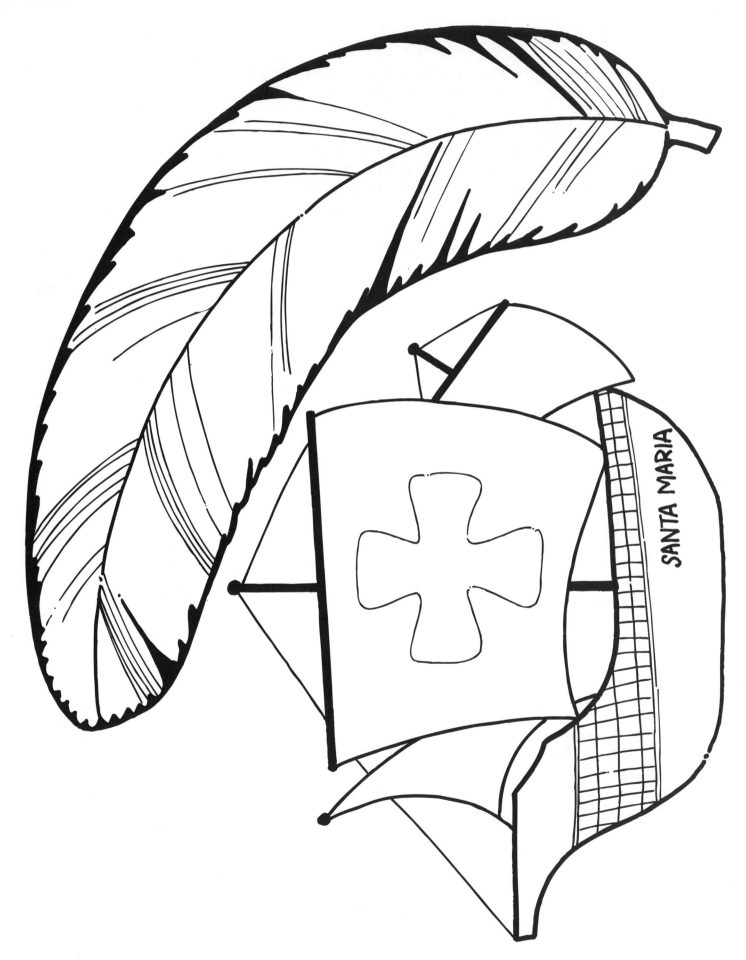

SANTA MARIA

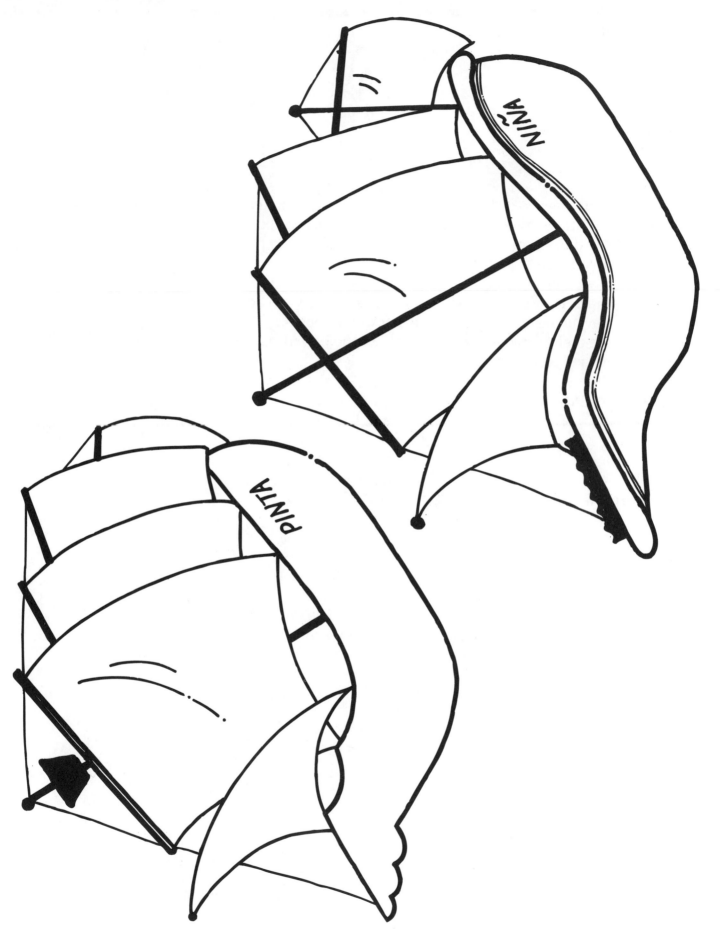

FALL CARRY-HOME FOLDERS

You need:
- crayons or markers
- scissors
- 10" x 13" construction paper
- glue
- stapler

1. Have each child choose two of the three patterns on pages 35 through 37. Reproduce both patterns for each child. Have children color and cut out.
2. Give each child two sheets of 10" x 13" construction paper. Have children glue one pattern on each sheet.
3. Have children place the two sheets of construction paper together so the patterns show on both sides. Help them staple along the sides and bottom of the sheets, leaving the top open to form a "pocket," as shown.
4. Children may use their fall carry-home folders to hold homework papers, notes to parents, and other items small enough to fit inside.

FALL BOOK COVERS

You need:
- crayons or markers
- scissors
- 12" x 18" art paper (any color)
- glue
- tape

1. Reproduce one pattern of choice from pages 35 through 37 for each child. Have children color and cut out.
2. Give each child a 12" x 18" sheet of art paper. Help them fold down both the top and bottom edges of the paper to fit the height of their book, as shown. For example, a 1 1/2" fold at both the top and the bottom of the paper will leave a 9" high cover.
3. Help children fold down the left and right edges of the paper to fit the width of their book. Slip each book cover into the fold of the paper, as shown. You may also wish to tape down the edges of the cover so it holds more securely.
4. Have children glue their pattern onto the front of their book cover.

Fall Pattern

Fall Pattern

ALL ABOUT LEAVES

Invite children to tell what they know about leaves. Then share the following information about leaves with the class.

• Leaves make food for plants so the plants can grow. Leaves need three things to make food: sunlight, water, and air. Plants store food made by leaves in their roots, stems, seeds, and fruits. Without this food, a plant could not live, just as people could not live without food.

• Leaves come in all shapes and sizes. There are three main kinds of leaf edges: smooth, toothed, and rounded. (Display the leaf patterns from the bottom of the page to help children see the three kinds of leaf edges.) Most leaves are about 1 to 12 inches long. The smallest leaves, which grow on asparagus plants, are so tiny that they can only be seen with a magnifying glass. The largest leaves, which grow on the African raffia palm, are 65 feet long! That's taller than ten men standing on each other's shoulders!

• Leaves are important to animals and people. Animals and people depend on plants for food, and plants could not grow without leaves. Also, leaves release oxygen into the air, which people and animals must breathe in order to live.

• Besides making food, leaves help plants in other ways. Some kinds of leaves have special layers that help protect the rest of the plant. Some leaves store food after making it. Some leaves are shaped so they help hold climbing plants in place. And still other leaves attract pollinating insects to the flower, or capture insects that the plant then eats.

• Leaves are also used by gardeners to help the soil stay healthy. Leaves serve as mulch, which is spread over the soil so that air can get through without letting the water in the soil evaporate. Leaves used as mulch also reduce the number of weeds that might otherwise grow in a garden and keep plants from growing there.

PRESERVING LEAVES

You need:
• freshly cut leaves
• newspaper
• books
• cardboard or construction paper
• tape

1. Inform children that freshly cut leaves will curl, dry up, and eventually crack if left alone. However, the leaves can be preserved by pressing them.
2. Have each child take a freshly cut leaf and put it between several sheets of newspaper.
3. Have children place a flat, heavy weight on the newspaper, such as a stack of books.
4. Let the books stay put for a week. Then remove them and let children retrieve their leaves, which will now remain flat.
5. Children can mount their leaves on cardboard or construction paper, placing a strip of tape across the stem to hold it in place.

MAKING LEAF RUBBINGS

You need:
• leaves
• tracing paper or thin typing paper
• soft pencils, charcoals, or wax crayons

1. Have children each take a leaf and lay it underside-up on a table. Then cover the leaf with a sheet of tracing paper or thin typing paper.
2. Have children quickly but gently rub the paper with the side of a sharpened soft pencil, a wax crayon, or a piece of charcoal.
3. When the entire leaf has been rubbed, children will see the outline and larger veins of the leaf imprinted on their paper.

OCTOBER HOLIDAY BOOKMARKS

You need:
- glue
- oaktag
- scissors
- crayons or markers
- collage materials
- clear contact paper

1. Reproduce the October bookmarks on pages 41 through 43 for each child. Have children mount the bookmarks on oaktag and cut out.
2. Encourage children to color and decorate their bookmarks using collage materials.
3. Help children laminate their bookmarks.
4. For activities, see Fall for Reading Club on page 44.

Bookmark Patterns

Spooky Stories send me Soaring!

Happy Reading!

FALL FOR READING CLUB

You need:
• crayons or markers
• scissors
• glue
• 12" x 18" manila paper

1. Reproduce one Fall for Reading bookmark on pages 41 through 43 for each child.
2. Have children color the bookmarks and cut them out. Have each child glue the bookmark on a 12" x 18" piece of manila paper.
3. Suggest children title their posters "Fall Books." Let children write their names on their posters and make decorative borders, leaving plenty of space in the middle for writing, as shown.
4. Help children record the books they read on the posters throughout the fall.
5. Display the posters on a reading center wall or a bulletin board for all to see.
6. Parents may send notes listing the books their children read at home. As each poster is filled up, that child may take it home.

MY FAVORITE STORIES

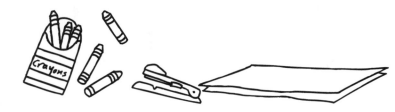

You need:
• drawing paper
• crayons or markers
• oaktag
• stapler

1. As part of the Fall for Reading Club, ask children to draw pictures and then write or dictate a few sentences about their favorite stories.
2. Have a discussion with children about their favorite stories. Ask children to bring in favorite books from home, or check them out of the library.
3. Display the books on a reading table and let children enjoy looking at them during free time.
4. Collect the pages. Cut two pieces of oaktag for front and back covers.
5. Staple the pages together, titling the book "Our Favorite Stories." Place the class book in the reading center for all to enjoy.

HALLOWEEN FIGURES HEADBANDS

You need:
- crayons or markers
- scissors
- stapler
- 2" x 24" strips of oaktag

1. Let each child choose a Halloween character from pages 46 through 48 to use for his or her headband. Reproduce the selected pattern for each child. Have children color and cut out.
2. Have each child staple the figure in the center of a 2" x 24" strip of oaktag, as shown.
3. Staple the headband to fit around each child's head.
4. For activities, see Halloween Singing Game on page 50.

Step 2

45

Halloween Headband Pattern

Cooperative Storytelling/Creative Writing

SPOOKY STORY BOX

You need:
• crayons or markers
• scissors
• medium-sized box
• construction paper
• glue
• 9" x 12" oaktag

1. Reproduce the Halloween headband figures on pages 46 through 48 for each child. Have children color and cut out.
2. Cover a medium-sized box with construction paper so that it resembles a haunted house. Have children glue yellow rectangles on the box to represent windows, as shown.
3. Fold a 9" x 12" piece of oaktag in half. Place the sheet on top of the box to make a roof, as shown.
4. Draw a 5" x 7" rectangle near the bottom of the box. Cut along two of the sides and fold the shape back, creating a door large enough for an adult hand to fit through.
5. Place the Halloween characters inside the door.
6. Have a small group of children sit in a circle, with the haunted house in the middle of the circle.
7. Invite one child to reach into the "haunted house" and pull out one of the figures. Ask another child to begin a Halloween story using that character.
8. Continue playing, allowing each child to remove another character from the haunted house. Encourage children to add to the story each time a new character is introduced.
9. If desired, ask the group to write or dictate their story and illustrate it to share with the rest of the class.

HALLOWEEN SINGING GAME

1. Have children wear their Halloween headbands and sit in a circle.
2. Teach children the following Halloween song. Ask those children wearing the Halloween character featured in the verse being sung to move around the outside of the circle, pantomiming how that character would act. Ask children to make up new verses about other Halloween characters.

Halloween Friends Song
(sung to the tune of "London Bridge")

Ghosts come out on Halloween,
Halloween, Halloween.
Ghosts come out on Halloween,
And float all around.

Repeat verses, substituting:

Cats prowl…
Bats swoop…
Monsters stomp…

HIDING ON HALLOWEEN

Name _____

Some Halloween friends are hiding on Halloween night. Are they afraid of the dark? Are they afraid of the trick-or-treaters? Find and circle the cat, bat, witch, ghost, and monster. Then color the picture.

Newbridge

51

HALLOWEEN DOORKNOB DECORATIONS

You need:
- crayons or markers
- glue
- oaktag
- scissors
- clear contact paper
- water-soluble markers
- hole puncher
- yarn

1. Let each child select a pattern on pages 53 through 55 to make a doorknob decoration. Reproduce the selected pattern once for each child. Have children color, mount on oaktag, and cut out.
2. Ask children to write a permanent message on the pattern, such as "Doreen's Room" or "Enter at Your Own Risk."
3. Use clear contact paper to laminate the doorknob decorations. If desired, have each child bring in a water-soluble marker to attach to the decoration with yarn so it may be used as a message board. Each child will need to punch a hole in the decoration, then tie one end of a length of 10" yarn to the marker and the other to the hole punched in the decoration.
4. Punch a hole in the top of the decoration, then tie a loop of yarn through. Children can use the loop to hang the decoration over their doorknob at home.

52

Spooky Cat Pattern

Bat Pattern

Pumpkin Pattern

HALLOWEEN STORIES

1. Have each child choose one pattern on pages 53 through 55 to use as the basis for a Halloween story. Reproduce the selected figure three times for each child.
2. Tell children to think up a story involving the selected figure. Make sure each story has three parts: a beginning, a middle, and an end.
3. Have each child glue the first figure to a piece of 12" x 18" construction paper and add background and other details using crayons or markers to create a setting for the story.
4. Help each child write or dictate a sentence that describes the beginning of his or her story.
5. Then have each child repeat steps 3 and 4 with the remaining two figures to tell the middle and end of the story.
6. When all the stories have been completed, help each child staple his or her story together along the left side in the correct order. Encourage volunteers to share their stories with the rest of the class.

HALLOWEEN CLASS DECORATION

1. Reproduce the pumpkin pattern on page 55 fourteen times. Have volunteers color and cut out.
2. Help children lay the pumpkins out in a row on the floor. Help children tape or glue the pumpkins together. You may also have children punch holes in each pumpkin stem and thread yarn through each pumpkin, as shown.
3. Lay out collage materials so children may personalize the pumpkins with hats, hair, and other decorations.
4. Write the letters for "Happy Halloween" across the figures. Attach the banner to a wall or a bulletin board.
5. Discuss with children rules to follow when trick-or-treating to have a safe and happy Halloween. Record the rules on experience chart paper and display near the banner.

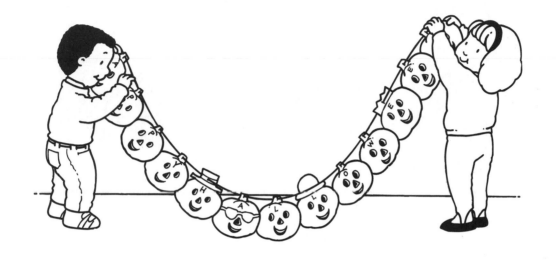

HALLOWEEN PARTY FAVORS

1. Distribute one cone-shaped cup and one large paper plate to each child.
2. Show children how to place the cup upside down on the paper plate and trace a circle, as shown.
3. Have children paint the cup and circle black so they look like the top and brim of a witch's hat. Leave the area where the cup was traced white. When dry, give children small treats to put into the cups. Help each child center the cone-shaped cup on the plate, covering the white area, and tape in place, as shown.
4. Children may bring the Halloween favors home or give to a friend.

GHOST FLASH

1. Reproduce the ghost pattern on page 59 ten times. On each ghost, write a number from one to ten.
2. Gather a group of three to four children together. Let one child select one of the ghosts and hold it up for three seconds so that the other children can see it. Then have the child put the ghost facedown on his or her lap. The other children then say the number they saw on the ghost.
3. For added challenge, use higher numbers. Older children may wish to make up addition or subtraction sentences to match the numbers on the ghosts.

GHOSTLY COLOR GAME

1. Reproduce the ghost pattern two or three times for each color you will be reviewing. Have volunteers color each ghost a different color.
2. Tape the ghosts on the floor randomly in a large open space. Demonstrate how to walk around the ghosts without touching them. Play spooky music while the children walk around the ghosts like monsters.
3. Stop the music suddenly and call out a color. Children must go to that color and touch it with their feet. (Encourage children to help each other fit on the ghost.)

Ghost Pattern

HALLOWEEN COLOR WHEEL

You need:
• crayons or markers
• scissors
• construction paper
• brass fasteners
• glue
• tape

1. Reproduce the ghost on page 59 once for each child. Have children color and cut out. Then reproduce the patterns on pages 62 and 63 twice for each child. Have children tape the pieces together to form a circle.
2. Tell children to color seven ghosts each a different color: blue, red, yellow, green, orange, purple, and black. Leave one ghost on each color wheel white.
3. Show children how to trace the large circle onto construction paper and cut out. Then help each child cut out a wedge-shaped triangle, as shown. The triangle should be the same size as each ghost wedge.
4. Have each child place the construction paper circle on top of the color ghosts circle and attach with a brass fastener, as shown.
5. Tell each child to glue the large ghost onto the construction paper wheel, as shown.
6. Demonstrate how to turn the bottom wheel so the color ghosts appear in the opening of the top wheel.
7. Ask children to turn the wheel and name the colors they see. Or, have them find a color you name by giving them a clue about the color. For example, you might say, "I am thinking of a color that you see on fire trucks." Then children can turn their color wheels to reveal the color red.

DECODING A GHOST MESSAGE

1. Ask volunteers to help assemble a Halloween Color Wheel on page 60.
2. Before school starts each day, think of a simple eight-word sentence. Write each word of the sentence on a 1" x 2" piece of white paper.
3. Attach the words in random order to the ghosts on the color wheel.
4. Cut out a 4" x 6" piece of construction paper for each of the eight colors featured on the color wheel.
5. Find the first word of the sentence on the color wheel. Place the corresponding piece of colored paper on a chalkboard. (For example, if the first word of the sentence is "The," and this word is located on the orange portion of the color wheel, the first piece of colored paper on the chalkboard should be orange.) Then find the second word of the sentence on the color wheel and place the corresponding color to the right of the first piece of colored paper. Continue until all eight pieces of colored paper are placed in sentence order across the chalkboard.
6. Tell children that the colored paper on the chalkboard is really a secret code. During free time, let children turn the wheel to "decode" the words in the sentence.
7. When children have decoded the message, have them check their answers with you.

What's the secret message?

Today   we   are   to   have   party

Ghost Color Wheel Pattern

Ghost Color Wheel Pattern

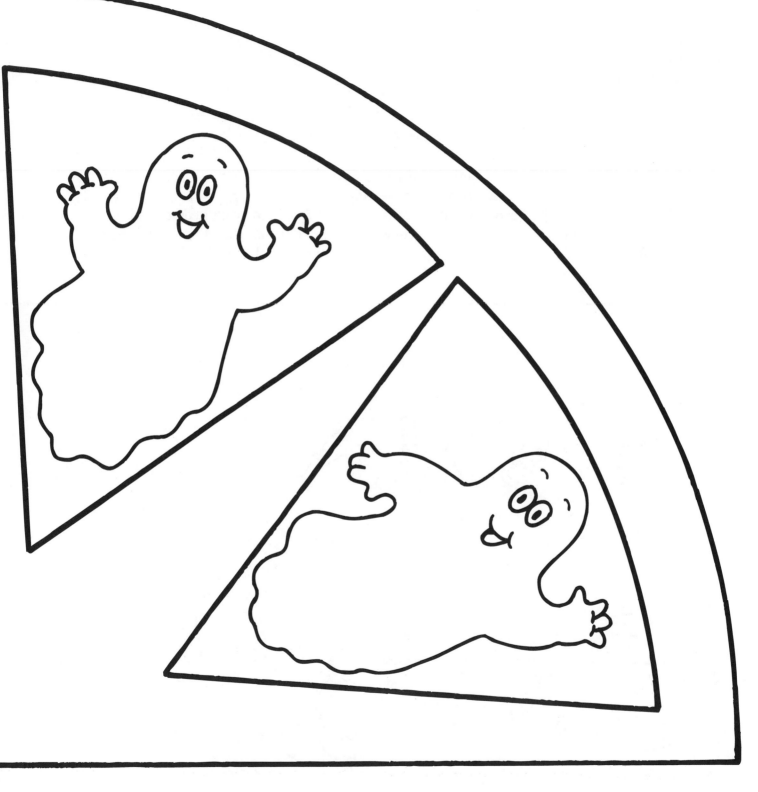

HALLOWEEN CAT PIÑATA

You need:
• crayons or markers
• scissors
• glue
• stapler
• wrapped candy and inexpensive prizes
• hole puncher
• strong cord or fishing line

1. Reproduce the cat head, body, and tail patterns on pages 66 through 68 twice. Reproduce the leg patterns on page 68 four times. Color one set of patterns, front and back. Cut out.
2. Glue the pieces together, as shown.
3. Place the front and back of the cat together and staple around the edges, leaving the tail free and keeping a small space near the top of the cat's head open, as shown.
4. Fill the cat with small wrapped candies and inexpensive prizes. Staple the cat's head closed.
5. Punch a hole in the cat's body and thread a piece of strong cord or fishing line through the hole.
6. Hang the cat from the ceiling just slightly above children's heads and play the Piñata Game at a class Halloween party.

PIÑATA GAME

1. Follow the directions on page 64 to create the Halloween Cat Piñata.
2. Hang the Halloween Cat Piñata from the ceiling just slightly above children's heads.
3. Have children stand in a circle at least three feet away from the piñata.
4. Choose one child to go first. Using the Spooky Cat Blindfold on page 69, blindfold the child and hand him or her a yardstick. Tell the child to use the yardstick to try to break open the piñata.
5. After the first child has hit the piñata once, blindfold another child and give him or her the yardstick. Continue around the circle until the piñata is broken. Then let the children take turns collecting the treats that fall.

CAT PARTY SANDWICHES

Have children make this snack for a class Halloween party.

You need:
• slices of bread
• 7- or 9-ounce paper cups
• plastic knives
• small paper plates or napkins
• peanut butter or cream cheese
• raisins
• pretzels

1. Show children how to cut a circle from a slice of bread by placing a 7- or 9-ounce paper cup upside down on the bread and cutting around it with a plastic knife. Using the remaining bread, help children form two triangles for the cat's ears, as shown.
2. Have children arrange their cat faces on small paper plates or napkins.
3. Let children spread peanut butter or cream cheese over the bread and then make cat faces using raisins for eyes and noses, pretzels for whiskers, and so on.
4. Encourage children to show others their cat faces before snacking on the sandwiches.

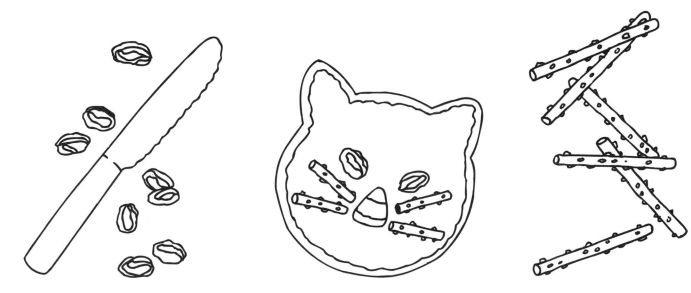

Cat Head Pattern

Cat Body Pattern

Cat Tail and Leg Patterns

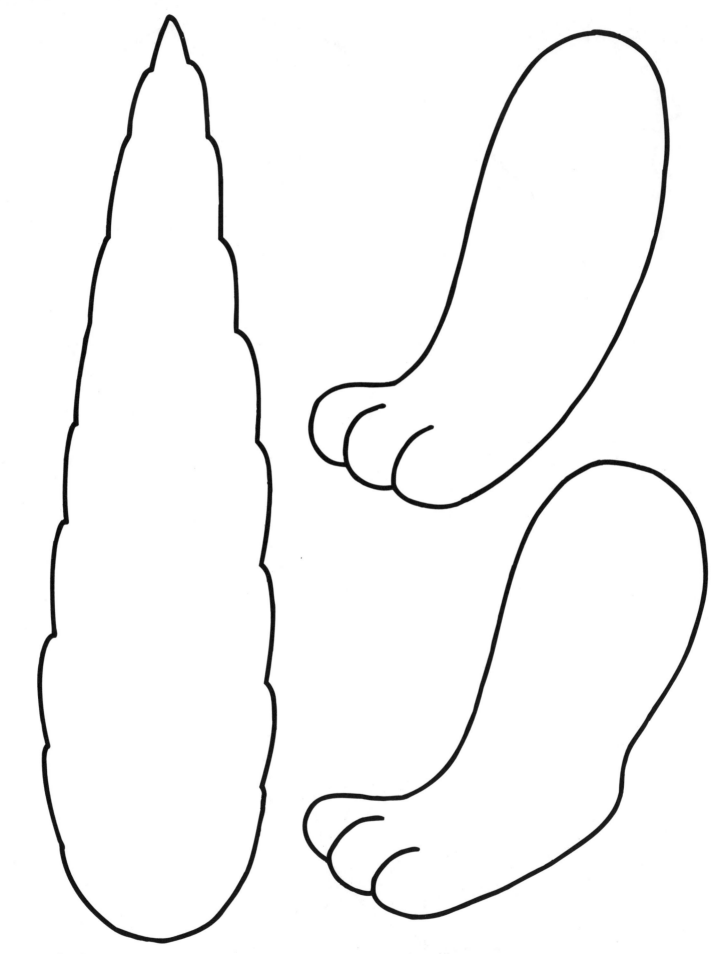

SPOOKY CAT BLINDFOLDS

You need:
• crayons or markers
• glue
• oaktag
• scissors
• hole puncher
• 12" pieces of string

1. Reproduce the cat face pattern on page 66 for each child. Have children color the faces, mount on oaktag, and cut out.
2. Help each child punch holes on either side of the face. Then show children how to thread a 12" piece of string through the holes to complete the blindfold.
3. For activities, see Pin the Tail on the Cat below, the Piñata Game on page 65, and the Fraidy-Cat Poem on page 70.

PIN THE TAIL ON THE CAT

You need:
• crayons or markers
• scissors
• glue
• construction paper
• masking tape
• pushpins or tacks

1. Reproduce the cat patterns on pages 66 through 68 once. Color and cut out.
2. Glue the pieces together, as shown. Do not attach the cat's tail.
3. Trace the tail on construction paper, making one tail for each child.
4. Have each child write his or her name on the tail. Tell each child to attach a piece of masking tape to the tail.
5. Mount the cat on a wall or bulletin board. Choose one child to go first and wear the Spooky Cat Blindfold. Have the child hold his or her tail, and then spin the child around once or twice.
6. Have the child move forward toward the cat and try to place the tail where it should go on the cat.
7. Continue until everyone has had a turn. The winner is the one whose tail has been placed closest to the appropriate place on the cat.

FRAIDY-CAT POEM

Reproduce the following choral poem for children. Divide the class into two groups and give each a cat part. Help children cut out the eyeholes in their blindfolds to create cat masks, and have them wear the masks as they practice their parts. After working with each group, have the whole class try the choral reading together.

Cat 1: Little Cat, why do you shiver with fright?

Cat 2: I am afraid 'cause it's Halloween night.

Cat 1: Are you afraid of ghosts in the air?

Cat 2: I'm not afraid of ghosts anywhere!

Cat 1: Are you afraid of pumpkins that glow?

Cat 2: No, I like them—that just isn't so.

Cat 1: Well, then, Little Cat, what do you fear?

Cat 2: It always happens this time of year...
        When sweet little children dress up and go out.
        They eat lots of candy. They scream and shout.
        It frightens me so to see them that way.
        I like them much better during the day!

Cat 1: Little Cat, why don't you curl up in a ball?
        If you fall asleep, you'll hear nothing at all.
        Halloween night will quickly pass.
        And the things you fear will be over at last!

THE TEENY TINY WOMAN FLANNEL BOARD

You need:
- oaktag
- crayons or markers
- scissors
- scraps of flannel or sandpaper
- glue
- flannel for a flannel board

1. Reproduce the flannel board patterns on pages 73 through 75. Have children mount on oaktag, color, and cut out.
2. Glue scraps of flannel or sandpaper to the back of each pattern.
3. Prepare a large flannel board that the patterns will adhere to.
4. Have volunteers move the patterns around as you read "The Teeny Tiny Woman" aloud.
5. During free time, let children play with the flannel board to create their own stories featuring the characters and objects from "The Teeny Tiny Woman."

THE TEENY TINY WOMAN FLANNEL BOARD STORY

Once upon a time, in a teeny tiny town, there lived a teeny tiny woman, a teeny tiny dog, and a teeny tiny cat. It was the night before Halloween. "I feel like taking a walk," said the teeny tiny woman. "Not a long walk, mind you. Just a teeny tiny walk." So the woman put on her teeny tiny coat and her teeny tiny hat, and she went outside. Of course, she took her teeny tiny dog and her teeny tiny cat along with her.

After a while, the teeny tiny woman came to a teeny tiny churchyard. She walked through the teeny tiny gate. Following right behind her were her teeny tiny dog and her teeny tiny cat. They all went into the teeny tiny churchyard and looked around. It was dark and spooky!

Suddenly, the teeny tiny woman saw something on the ground shining in the moonlight. It was a teeny tiny white bone. "Well, what do you know!" cried the teeny tiny woman in her teeny tiny voice. "A teeny tiny bone!" Suddenly, the teeny tiny dog began to bark. "What do you want?" asked the teeny tiny woman in her teeny tiny voice. "Oh, I see. You want me to give you this teeny tiny bone to play with." Then the teeny tiny cat began to meow. "And what do you want?" asked the teeny tiny woman in her teeny tiny voice. "Oh, I see. You want me to give you this teeny tiny bone, too." The teeny tiny dog and the teeny tiny cat both jumped up in the air.

"Well," said the teeny tiny woman, "neither of you will have this bone. For I shall take it home and make a teeny tiny soup." And so the teeny tiny woman put the teeny tiny bone in her teeny tiny purse and started to leave the teeny tiny churchyard. And, of course, following right behind her were her teeny tiny dog and her teeny tiny cat.

As they all walked home, the teeny tiny woman thought she heard a teeny tiny noise behind her. It sounded like rattling. She turned around, but saw nothing. The teeny tiny woman didn't know she was being followed by a teeny tiny skeleton!

When she got home, the teeny tiny woman took the teeny tiny bone from her teeny tiny purse and put it in the teeny tiny kitchen cupboard before going to sleep. The teeny tiny woman crawled into her teeny tiny bed. She didn't see the teeny tiny skeleton that was hiding behind her teeny tiny cupboard.

The teeny tiny woman fell asleep, but she was soon awakened by a teeny tiny voice calling out softly, "Give me back my bone! Give me back my bone!" The teeny tiny woman looked at her teeny tiny dog and said, "Is that you talking to me?" But the teeny tiny dog just shook its teeny tiny head no.

The teeny tiny woman tried to fall asleep again. But soon she heard the teeny tiny voice call out a little louder, "Give me back my bone! Give me back my bone!" The teeny tiny woman looked at her teeny tiny cat and said, "Is that you talking to me?" But the teeny tiny cat just shook its teeny tiny head no.

The teeny tiny woman began to get a teeny tiny bit scared. She pulled her teeny tiny blanket over her teeny tiny head and called, "Go away, whoever you are! I am not afraid of you!"

Suddenly, the teeny tiny skeleton jumped out from behind the teeny tiny cupboard. "GIVE ME BACK MY BONE!" it cried. "GIVE ME BACK MY BONE!" Now the teeny tiny woman was really scared! She jumped from her teeny tiny bed, ran to her teeny tiny cupboard, and took out the teeny tiny bone.

"Here!" cried the teeny tiny woman in her loudest teeny tiny voice. "Take your bone! AND GET OUT OF MY HOUSE!" The teeny tiny skeleton grabbed the teeny tiny bone and began to run off, making a teeny tiny rattling sound along the way. But before going through the teeny tiny front door, the teeny tiny skeleton turned to the teeny tiny woman and said, "I have just one more thing to say to you, teeny tiny woman. HAPPY HALLOWEEN!"

Teeny Tiny Woman Story Patterns

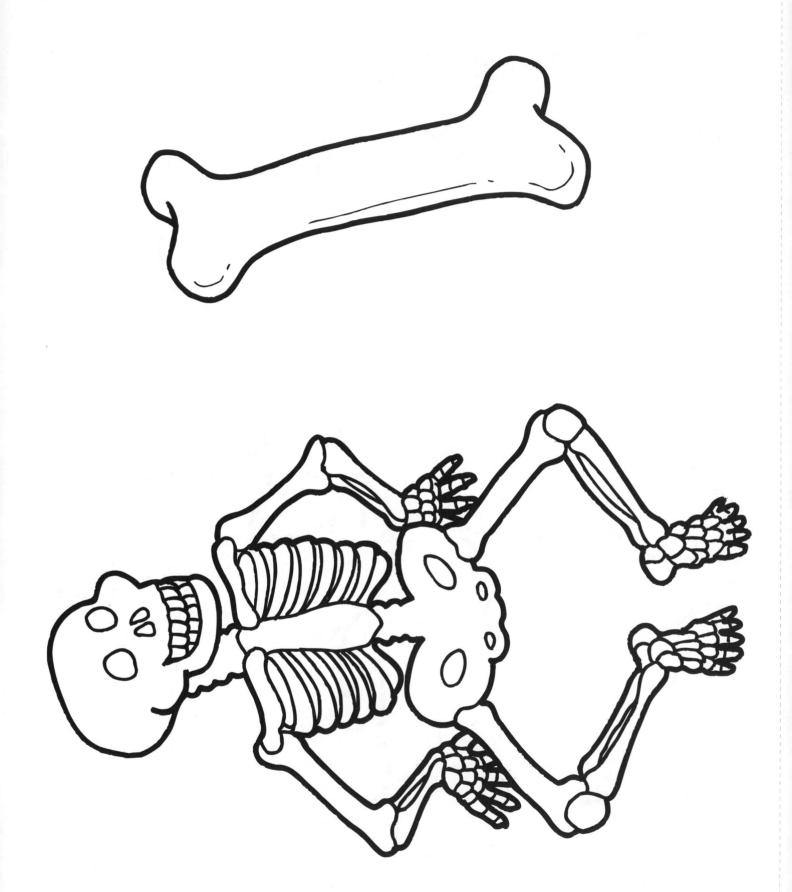

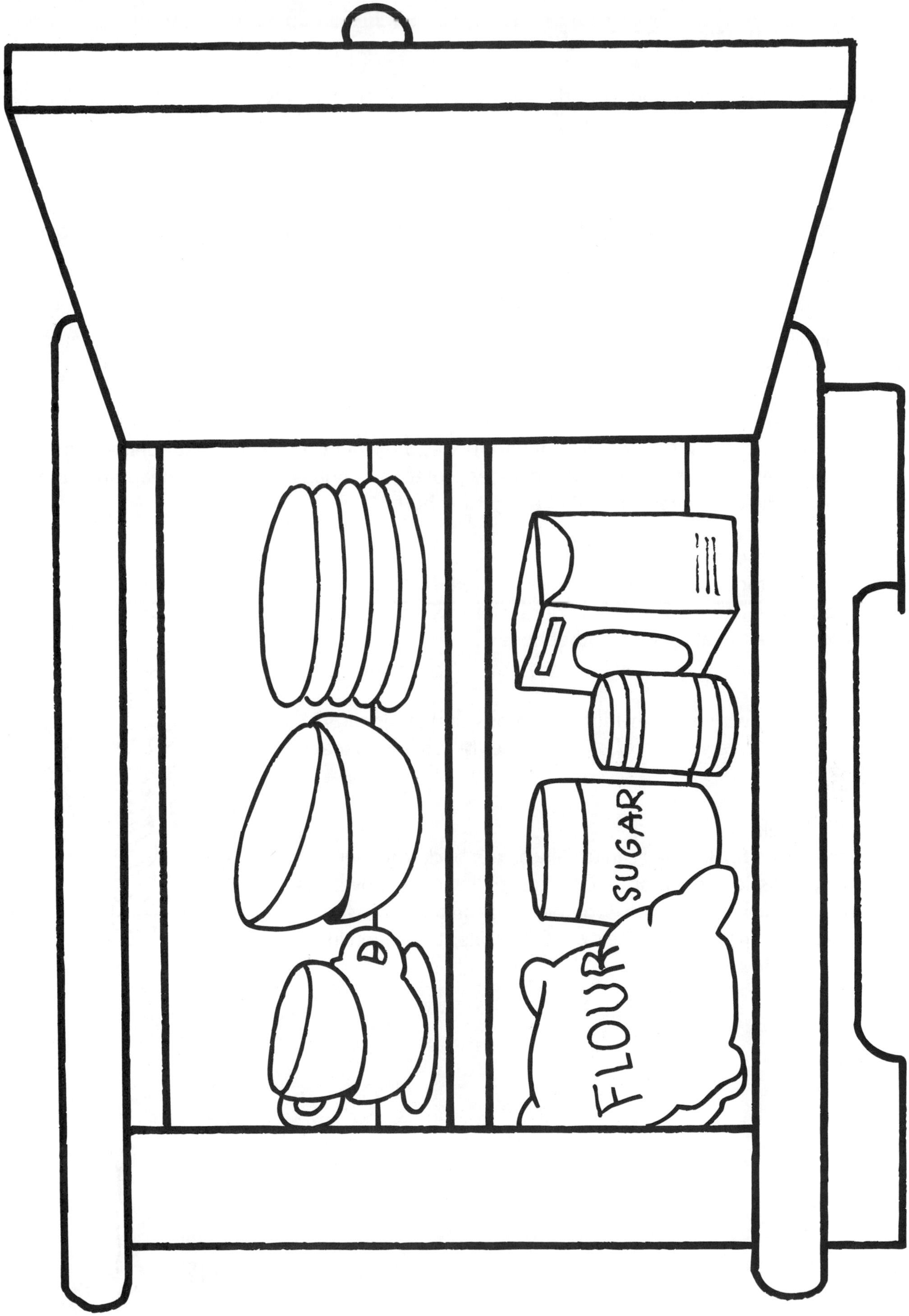
SUGAR
FLOUR

QUESTIONS AND ANSWERS ABOUT BONES

Have children write or dictate questions they have about bones. Then share the information below. Ask children to listen to hear if their questions are answered.

Q: What are bones made of?
A: Bones are made of material called tissue. A bone has two kinds of tissue. One kind is the hard, outside part of the bone. It is made of minerals. The other kind is the soft, spongy inside part. It is called marrow.

Q: Do all people and animals have bones?
A: All people have bones, and so do most animals. Some animals, such as worms, spiders, and octopuses, do not have bones. Insects such as flies and bees do not have bones either, but they have a skeleton made of other material that is actually lighter and stronger than bone.

Q: How do bones help us?
A: Bones help us move our bodies. If we did not have bones, we would flop around like spaghetti or a rag doll. Bones help us move our arms and legs. Some bones protect our organs, such as our heart and lungs. Our skull is the hard bone that keeps our brain from getting hurt.

Q: How do bones stay together?
A: Our bones are held together by tough, rubbery material called ligaments. Bones and ligaments make up our skeleton. Every bone in our body is connected to at least one other bone.

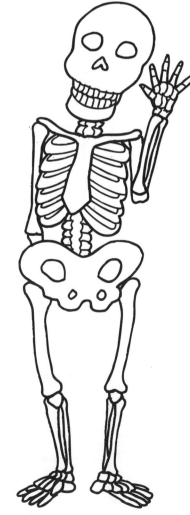

Q: Do bones grow?
A: Yes, they grow along with our skin, muscles, organs, and other parts of our body. Babies have very soft bones. Their bones become harder and bigger as they grow older.

Q: Do bones ever break?
A: Yes, sometimes they do. But they can usually be put back together. When a bone breaks, it is set, or placed in a cast so it will not move. The broken ends of the bone then grow together. This can take from four weeks to one year, depending on the size of the bone, its location in the body, and the person's age.

TEENY TINY RIDDLES

Invite children to work individually or with a partner to make up "teeny tiny" riddles with answers starting with the letter "t." Give these examples:

Riddle 1:   I am little. I hold water. People take a bath in me. What am I?
A teeny tiny tub.

Riddle 2:   I am little. I live in the jungle. I am orange with black stripes. What am I?
A teeny tiny tiger.

Riddle 3:   I am little. I chug along a track. People take rides on me. What am I?
A teeny tiny train.

Encourage volunteers to share their riddles. See how many classmates can guess the right answers.

HIDDEN BONES

Name _____

Circle the hidden bones in each picture.

Teacher's Notes

Teacher's Notes